PRAISE F

"I recommend reading ⌐
accompanied by a warn. _   .... poems .ing with the joy
of nature and the sweetness to be found in the ordinary moment.
As Jody Collins says in the preface, 'Annual cycles in our physical
world also mirror our interior lives,'—a point well made herein.
A teacher-poet, Jody's poems teach us to see, to hear, to notice our
lives and to let the simple gifts arriving in each common moment
move us to a place of praise and intimacy with God."

—Laura Boggess, author of *Playdates with God: Having a Childlike
Faith in a Grown-up World* and *Waiting for Neruda's Memoirs*

"Collins's work is deliberate, her cadence soothing. As I read, I find
myself taking in deeper breaths and sighing, everything slowing
around me. 'Bring the wind of your Spirit and build anew,' she
writes. Indeed. Except here the spirit arrives on the wind of her
words, and I can feel something new building inside of me."

—Shawn Smucker, author of *Light from Distant Stars*

"In *Hearts on Pilgrimage*, poet Jody Collins pays detailed attention to
our world and the language we use to describe it. At times playful,
always articulate, Collins skillfully weaves poems exploring the
overlap of our internal and external worlds of awareness and ob-
servation. Full of questions and patient listening, Collins writes our
hearts toward home with words that 'fly, lunar-drawn, to the sky.'"

—Kelly Chripczuk, author and speaker at thiscontemplativelife.org

"In *Hearts on Pilgrimage*, Jody Collins takes her readers on a journey
of delight and discovery. Each deftly rendered image—from doing
dishes in the dark to listening to birdsong—paints a portrait of
the mysteries that lie just beyond our reach. Full of warmth and
insight, Collins's poems invite you to take a seat at the table, drink
deeply of everyday moments and enter the presence of God."

—Laura Kauffman, author of *Carolina Clay: A Collection of Poems
on Love and Loss*

"The poems of *Hearts on Pilgrimage* find the sacred in the every-day—a spider's web, the music of the wind, the pattern in the sky, a flower in a field. But Collins does more: She sees, with a poet's eye, the everyday holiness of the image in an ultrasound, the voice of a grandchild, and the natural process of aging. The collection is an exercise in startling stillness."

—**Glynn Young, contributing editor at Tweetspeak Poetry and author of the five *Dancing Priest* novels and *Poetry at Work***

"In her newest release, *Hearts on Pilgrimage: Poems & Prayers,* Jody Collins offers readers a beautifully crafted and artfully organized collection. This work invites readers onto the page as pilgrims on a seasonal journey of becoming aware—aware of both God's presence and His created beauty. Collins's poems and prayers come from an earthy richness, born from the soil of profoundly personal storytelling as she unearths the world around her. Each work meets us in our own humanity as cosojourners, where poems are readable, relatable and approachable in their crafting. Well-written and well-timed in its release into the world, *Hearts on Pilgrimage* is the perfect antidote for the world of 2020 and beyond, for it is a book of hope."

—**Elizabeth Marshall, writer at elizabethmarshall.com**

"In *Hearts on Pilgrimage: Poems & Prayers,* Jody Collins delights in things most of us take for granted—the ruby postscript of a raspberry, the honeyed breeze of dawn, and chip-clacking juncos. She ponders single pantry ingredients shelved in the dark—safe but isolated. Collins carves her heart on and houses hope in these pages, inviting us to find our own balance in beauty and to seek God's presence in every season."

—**Sandra Heska King, Community Care and Social Media at Tweetspeak Poetry, photographer and writer at sandraheskaking.com**

"Collins had me at the word 'Pilgrimage.' Wrapped in the certain rhythm of seasons, she lends us her eyes to see the wonder and everyday beauty of dishes in the dark or a baby bird's first solo flight. Whatever season you're in, Jody's soulful words will meet you with comfort, hope, and joy for your journey."

—**Kim Hyland, author of *An Imperfect Woman: Letting Go of the Need to Have It All Together* and founder of Winsome Living**

Hearts on Pilgrimage

Poems & Prayers

HEARTS
ON
PILGRIMAGE

POEMS & PRAYERS

Jody L. Collins

Published by Newport Press, Renton, Washington.
jodyleecollins.com

Cover artwork watercolor by Laura Winslow,
laurawinslow.blogspot.com.

Author photo by Kris Camealy.

Cover and interior book design by Mi Ae Lipe, whatnowdesign.com.

Printed in the United States of America.

To contact the author for permissions or order additional copies:
jodyleecollins.com

First Edition, 2021

ISBN: 978-1-7362774-1-6

Library of Congress Control Number: 2020922694

For who knows how,
Better than he that taught us first to Plough,
To guide our Mind and Pens for his Design?
And he makes base things usher in Divine.

—John Bunyan—
from the *Author's Apology* for his book

This page is soil
ground coarse to fine.

Daily life returning self to soul,
back to owning that which is mine,
Savior always mending whole.

The work is His; my words have told
dull beauties, His love the foil.

CONTENTS

Act II: Spring—Sowing & Hope

Act III: Summer—Move & Grow

PREFACE

The Path

When I said my initial *yes* to Jesus over 40 years ago, I found poet Luci Shaw's first book, *Listen to the Green*, and was overcome with the "perhapses" and possibilities of being a poet. I am adept at saying way more than is needed to communicate a point. What would happen, I wondered, if I intentionally pared down my words to say more with less? *Listen to the Green* was the inspiration and beginning of my journey into poetry.

I managed to scribble random lines, gathering thoughts in the margins of my days between chasing children and teaching school. Most of it was very bad "poetry," but it was a start. As I chose to grow and learn, I invested in an informal education—"The School of 3,000 Books," as poet Barbara Crooker would say. The volume you now hold in your hands is the fruit of that learning, a culmination of inspiration and encouragement from poets I've had the pleasure of reading and learning from along the way. These poets include Laurie Klein, Scott Cairns, Malcolm Guite, Luci Shaw and many others.

The Process

When I began the draft of *Hearts on Pilgrimage*, it was early spring 2020. I had been approached by a friend about placing my poems in her care for their possible publication. After a time of waiting and listening, the work landed back in my lap while our collective lives were put on permanent pause by the entry of a disruptive and devastating virus. Life in the time of corona has wreaked havoc on life as we know it. *Knew it.*

I will never look at spring the same way again, but I am hopeful. And that is the purpose of spring—God's eternal message that new life will come from what seems lifeless and gone. Winter's barrenness provides a creation backdrop that speaks to God's presence in the middle of life when everything has been stripped away, and no year illustrates this truth more than this one.

The Poems

Annual cycles in our physical world also mirror our interior lives, whether or not we are conscious of it. When I sat with these poems, they organized themselves in a way that began with winter and its time of dormancy and rest, moving through spring bringing new life, to summer with its burgeoning growth and flourishing, and into autumn with an eye towards harvest and a future. The Church year, beginning as it does in the very last days of November, also takes us through this cycle of winter, spring, summer and fall. *Hearts on Pilgrimage* follows this path. My liturgical friends may recognize a poem for Good Friday and Pentecost Sunday.

The book's title came from a phrase in George Herbert's poem "Prayer" and a line in Psalm 84:5, which says, "Blessed are those whose strength is in you, whose hearts are set on pilgrimage." I made the note about Psalm 84 in 2007 and wrote "Book title?" next to the verse. George Herbert's poem came into my life many, many years later and the Spirit's echo sounded again. The phrase seemed to fit this work perfectly.

The Particulars

Nearly half of the poems are anchored in creation—my garden, the trees outside, birds that visit our feeders, the night sky. Someone once said, "Nature is God's noisiest orator," and I have found this to be true, writing most often about what I see and hear. I've also woven in the mundane alongside the miraculous, from making coffee in the kitchen to doing dishes in the dark. There are poems about children in the sprinklers, picking raspberries and a cruet of oil, all crafted with an eye that sees God's invisible Kingdom.

I began the book's sequence with an "Opening Act," setting the stage with reflections on writing and prayer. Sections that follow are Act I: Winter—Waiting & Still; Act II: Spring—Sowing & Hope; Act III: Summer—Move & Grow; and Act IV: Fall—Harvest & Future. The book ends with Act V: Coming & Going, with a look to the past as well as forward.

It should be noted many of these poems first appeared on my website or in other publications, both online and in print. Some of them are featured here for the first time.

I write primarily in free verse, but also play with rhyme and meter a bit, which was a delight to try. George MacDonald's classic *Diary of an Old Soul* (1880) provides inspiration for the cycle of five seven-line poems included here, and I've also written two sonnets in loosely rendered form. Initially intimidated by the constraints of the pattern, I was surprised at the freedom provided in writing within prescribed boundaries; it was fun to play around with the words.

My Prayer

Publishing a book of poetry, noticing the good, true and beautiful, seems a fruitless endeavor in the midst of challenges and heartache. But we will always have trouble and sorrow with us. While we live in a fallen world, we live with a risen Savior, and God's invisible Kingdom is there for us to see if we are looking. In every season we journey through, what draws us on is an awareness of God's beauty and presence.

As you read this work through the year or match it to your current season, I pray you will find an echo of our Creator's voice while walking your own path. There is much to behold, and I look forward to pointing the way, showing you what I see and hear. Then I hope you'll find time to jot your own poetic thoughts in the margins.

We are all on pilgrimage. Come walk with me?

Jody Collins
September 2020

Pilgrimage

Since I am coming to that holy room ...
I shall be made thy music. —John Donne

Our journey home begins
daily with the sun. And a map.
Oriented by true north, that
compass which magnets
us in subtle, insistent ways, we move.
Deep and invisible, His song draws
us on as we come 'round again
in a thousand turns to the sound
of that voice.
We are *Peregrinus*, pilgrims
wandering place to place,
straining for an echo of melody,
words to a song we forgot we knew.
Forever we crease and fold our maps,
spilling tea as we travel, stain and blur
lines as we learn the way.
We look up. Scan the signs,
slow down, take note.

―――――

No. Not a map, a musical score,
vellum notes traced over time
played on heart's harp, tuning
our ears ever more finely to the
pitch, not of His voice, but His tent,
that dwelling place where we finally
meno with Him. Home at last.

OPENING ACT

SETTING THE STAGE

Contemplate

I've no chisel but this pen
chipping at paper like stone,
carving words, not to build but bend
graphite like steel, curve the bones
(Dear God, not break) but lay in place
and then form a space to hold a new
edifice, sculpt and rest and tap some more
while You hand me bricks to begin, restore.

Grammar

The world's replete with prepositions. Speech
parsed just so bids me gaze beyond my reach
beneath, within, away and through
illimited by my feet and the earthbound view—
words, phrases, paragraphs written on the blue.
Rabbi's voice reminds that parables abound
above, and here where I walk, the ground
reveals to my attentive gaze the Kingdom
awaits in mossy cracks and rain-dript ways
penned with earthly sights and sounds.

Roguish clouds play at the edge of sky
write of a kingdom beyond my sight
luring my vision over sodden ground, high
atop feathered evergreens where God is found.

How to Write a Poem
after Wendell Berry

Create something with your hands,
occupy the space in which you live.
Stand still and stare through
morning glass.
Hold with two hands your steaming
cup and sip while listening
to the avian symphony embellishing
the day. Find a space of quiet, if
not without, within, deep breaths
moving you to a spacious place,
not unlike this blank page.
Then pick up your pen and begin.

Morning Percussion

The crow whose *caw, caw, caw,* Webster's
reference for the word "cacophony," brazenly
announces the day, surveys these early morning
woods from pencil-thin fir branch. Fog-shrouded
neighbor lumbers along behind homestead
compost bin, its percussive, *rumblety-bump,*
rumblety-bump rippling the air as it meets my ears.
Shrill scales and insistent cries surround my covered
space as dawn's alarm crescendos courtesy
of bluejay, chickadee, nuthatch, robin.

An early morning jet diagonals the sky,
sound surges into view. Anchored by
the constant companion of my patio
clock, time ticks its background as I begin,
pen across the page and record
my quiet thoughts in the key of day.

Listening Between the Lines

Which side of the brain remembers a recipe?
Hefty volume opened on my lap deckside, words
stand proud of the page conveying some salubrious
delight or another. Skin registers a delicious breeze,
tasting cool in every pore, then distraction lights
like a sudden butterfly. Now engaged, the opposite
brain-side finds the outdoor soundtrack—
an ice cream truck's water-torture tune
the *scree, scree, scree!* of a red flicker
faraway drum of a speedboat on the lake
tick, tick, click of the kitchen clock
the incessant neighborhood tune of children at twilight.

Though I've scanned ingredients, directions,
pertinent comments, what I deftly recall is the whisper
of jeweled water from the patio fountain woven
underneath the air's night noise. Listening tight
to the ruffled air feeds me best, nourishing music
a sound for my thirsty ears. I squash the urge
to cook—in this heat? Never!—Close the cookbook
and scribble this poem instead righting
the recipe Heavenward.

Parts of Speech

Now Let And Yet
How can the power
of my surrender
be wrapped tight
in three slight letters?
And yet.
Placed just so like fine
crystal, words refract
evening sun into shards
of light, precede each sentence,
illuming my way
to the next best *yes.*

Prayers on Paper

I write by faith, graphite gracing the
white, going somewhere. Pictures
appear like the slow and certain advent
of an image in a dark room. As solution
is exposed to its subtle Source, revelation
unfurls. Like the artist, I hold paper in hand
committing to discovery as I hold my
wordmap up to the light of day
and everything slowly becomes clear.

The First Lesson
for Scott Cairns

I sweep my net in the air waves,
    strain sound through
    the sieve in my hand,
    holding, not water—impossible—
    but a weight nonetheless
    of words as I swim through
    this world.
I dive deep in shallows,
    fingerholds on pebbles large
    and small as I excavate
    stones to build a sentence,
    or perhaps a pearl to
    string along.
Told to trust the safety
    net of language,
    I glean and gather,
    notice the way light lands
    just so, opaque enough
    for a poem to pass through.
So I lace the page, a necklace
    fashioned with cultured
    grains of sand, sifted, sewn
    between the lines, gathered
    in a velvet purse, buried
    treasure for others to lift
    and hold to the light.

Viewfinder

Sitting with a predawn view
to silhouetted hills through
the scrim of trees, a crayon
kaleidoscope, eyes reach the
blank white/blue of horizon.
Light competes for sky space
with evergreens branching skyward
while the juncos ponder breakfast
in the still, cool air. Perhaps they're
waiting for more nature noise,
a leaf-green, branch-wise twig-sound
to accompany their first meal of the day.
I feast on mine—teakettle's
slow rumble, the metronome
of clock, with pen in hand, eyes
on the page. Focused on
the meal before me is enough
for now. Let the world wake up later.
I am writing.

Write Here

Glittering beetles punctuate
the horizon, wink in sunlight
as they wend their way Somewhere.
Stationery, I glance through glass,
wonder at their homeward their hurry
while luxury affords me this stillness.
Gifted with time, free for the moment
no longer drawn by duty to be
Elsewhere, I write from my chair
instead, grateful for the sparkle
of sunshine on snow outside
my window and this spark
inside right here.

Writer's Break

I've been awash in words of late, missing
out on wind waving through slate-colored
branches against a Delft sky. Eyes too crowded
to take note of the weather which goes on without
me, whether I watch it or not.

A glance through the dining room glass
amplifies my loss in all caps. I pause.
There is no earth-changing script
worth attending that compares to
lines written in a twilight-borne
horizon this early March evening.
My heart listens to whispers without
words, memory deposited for
another day.
Banking on the Spirit's call, I pray
for better hearing, pay attention
to the tune, sharpen my gaze
along with my pencil. Freshly
scribbled notes sing
from the page, grace this
nascent composition, fly
towards the Heavens.

ACT I

WINTER

WAITING & STILL

After Clarice

a light rain is falling.
perhaps, like the trace of a breeze
it will bring a fresh spirit of peace
to a world that's imploding.
shattered seeds scatter, float
soft and silent as dandelion tufts
over this particular curve
of earth, to settle after the
whispers have died away,
the sobs have sounded.

Now quicken each shell with
impossible life where death
has sought its place.
Overtake like greenshoot vines,
defiant in destruction's face,
willing the water of too many
tears to reign deep in
the dark where, in time,
these lives will heave their
way to the light once again.

Doing Dishes in the Dark

I wash by touch, a tactile exchange
 for the gift of this misted view
 illumined by the morning's
 solar accompaniment.
After countless days of practice, I can scrub
 plates with my eyes closed.
If I flip on the lights my task is sealed; drudgery
 ahead. I'm formally present and engaged
 in keeping house.
But what keeps me?
A window to the world beyond my sink and suds,
 a looking glass invitation to gaze and rest
 my heart-eyes on the horizon
God-breathed and framed, hung just high enough,
 beckoning attention to this gossamer
 morning where, soon enough,
 I will be present and formally engaged.
Water runs.
 I rinse and stack by heart, a silent sigh
 registering the sight before me, sating
 my senses as I come to mine,
Grateful for hands that read silver, recognize
 glass, surrender to suds as I translate
 the day to come.

Isaiah 1:18

Snow comes, unexpected like
grace after a fall (yours, mine,
ours) a quiet wool covering
missteps, mistakes, messes.
White-soft gift leaves an expanse
of peace, pulling my eyes away
from the ground, these humble,
human feet, to misty, gray horizon.
Heart now centered, sheltered, still
where Creation whispers my thanks.

January Bird

Where have you been?
Out of town like those who flee
our chilled clime and metallic skies?
Elsewhere, warming up your voice
to herald today's sunrise with your song?
I welcome your morning melody
making its way to my ears,
stirring memories of other songs
on sullen, silver days when your music
was my only companion, a balm
for the emptiness at the edge
of my days.

Lighthouse

I wish I could collect
the light landing shadows
on this page as it creeps
ever brighter through the gray.
Pour it out to wash my heart,
salve the wound of this
present heaviness, sighs
that never end. Hold it lightly
aloft, praying no sharp wind
or quiet, steady breeze snuff
it out, for we need it so.

Father, carry us, ferry
us through storms,
humble, silent and still
as we shine hope in the right
direction—people-ward,
upward. Send us, spread us
like the daily sure rising
of your sun, that moves ever
on in the distant dark.

Slow

Warming bowl in hand, I rediscover my
favorite place. Well-worn, faded overstuffed
chair with its just-right fit, veiled light over
my left shoulder, the way the nearby clock
measures the morning. I ponder the truth—
I cannot eat on the run. Well, shouldn't.

I chafe at the need to be still, notice I am wont
to stuff my time like this chair, cushioned
to comfort me, held close as a glove.
But cushioned and comfortable leaves me closed—
dull to sights, deaf to hidden sound, safe from feeling.

So I reckon with the light, take note of my need to behold,
not be held, to live open to my senses, awake
to visions and voices, the day's illumination.
I savor the taste of raisins, crunch of grain, warmth
of milk and glance across the room towards
the light, grateful for a tongue to taste, eyes to see
and a heart to hear the day.

Thresh Hold

We are held as we pass through
doorways, daily sifted to see
what to carry, what to leave
as we look at the nascent view,
vaguely aware of the Voice calling
us on amid the sifting, the shifting
of ground beneath our feet.

Forcing new awareness, joy
bubbles through broken surfaces
of soil beneath our feet.
We move on. We are held.

Traveling

When two have trod this
valley of the shadow,
death coming anyway
          but not to you
and there is breath to greet
each day, just barely.
When your soul
is shredded to its core,
dreams buried in
handfuls of dirt
that frozen day,
all other storms
man-made or God-breathed
          like snow
prove anew another
way to open the sky
while you climb,
survivors towards the sun.

Work. Out.

for Anne Overstreet

Prayers rise or seep perhaps,
pushing their way through
arms as I pump my way to health.
I am petition in motion, wordless
sentence, like fog enveloping terrain
uneven as the surface of the brain.
Or the moon. I cast my thoughts there,
above and far beyond this gray day
praying for one particular gray
that matters. Words fly,
lunar-drawn, to the sky.

Sabbath on the Page, Winter

What can you hear
    in a winter sky? Trees
    as they sleep, sap as it
    rises, slowly stopped by
    these northern climes
    and their accompanying chill.
The sound of sunlight, settled
    like a theater's best ending,
    shadowplay reserved for
    juncos and chickadees.
Gray like warm flannel on a
    winter's night by the
    fire, celestial feathers
    cover like a goose's wing
    over her chicks.
I tune my pencil, painting
    this poem of treesound,
    cloudstill and year's end,
    while I listen
    for tomorrow's song.

ACT II

SPRING

SOWING & HOPE

Conditioned Air

Breeze rushes through greenscape
    on its way inside
Chlorophyll carrying cool to my overwarm
    skin.
Greensong lifts on the brass of garden
    chimes, sing with the wind as they
    wave a tune.
Breath, wind, spirit, Carrier of life
    as You brush across the water,
    alive with its moving, cool as a cave,
    refreshing as yesterday's rock-
    resting morning.

First Things—An Inventory

Does a light switch count as a thing
to be counted? Morning's first touch
is the "on" that brings light to amber-
colored floor and almost-yellow walls.
Next is the (obvious) electric tea kettle
empty (as always) awaiting its early
morning refill. Held under the faucet,
water pours in as I glance at the fill line
etched on the edge.

Is water a "thing" I wonder, as it vanishes
down drains, vaporizing via clouds? Given
its alchemic addition to coffee grounds,
a magic in these morning moments, I'd say
water is clearly a thing to be counted.
I mark its silver clarity in early light's
puddle at my feet, asterisk my entries.
Light and water.
They definitely count.

Leafworks

Like the bound bud in an almost-
bloomed magnolia, there is life
ready to burst, tight secrets
on the God side buried within
these cool, bright days.
I'm waiting, watching, counting
the sleeps until a quiet wonder
world awakens. Amazed,
I waltz between the longest watch
from each dormant doorway,
through the chill and darkened
mornings to a heart like an open gate.
Ear cupped, poised for my next
birth, I linger for delivery
of the morning's message—
free and God-breathed—
a silent, green unfurling.

Five Small Poems

Building

I am His body-house, master designed
My skin his indwelling, living walls
Word-breathed into being, built by His plan.
Transformed by Presence, this Architect calls
And cradles me; heart-close, my defenses fall.
Surrendered daily, my life expands,
He fills each room slowly, my All in All.

Perspective

Vision drawn down, not out beyond this space
Surmising what's here shows all that's seen.
Then pulled gently as a silken strand might
Hold, I view green and gold outside this place.
Eyes beholding leaf and bower, Creation's
Queens and kings hold forth, at rest, in flight
Fluttering then still, reflect day's soft light.

Vantage

Flat-bottomed magic, changing in thin air
Vapor, edge-shaped grows, billows, climbs high,
Draws vision over tree-tops mid-sky and dares
To rise beyond my eyes. I peer and sigh
Anchored, still, viewing from my earthly chair,
Ponder celestial science that rules the day
Ground me as its cumulus message fills the sky.

Garden

Raspberry jewels, fruited gems of this realm
Rich, deep red embeds earthly, emerald vines
I ponder that other kingdom laced with stones
Foundation gleaming like these garnets from
Heaven itself, plucked, eaten, freely mine.
Draping the edges of my garden home
Echoing borders of that celestial clime.

Growth

Does green hurt when the first time it appears
New-shot, bursting from winter's sodden gray
Unfurling like a ship piercing the waves?
I pioneer this day, breathe and press on
Through each step of glory, open but weak
Hold my life aloft, palmed in faith with fear
Ready and still, praise the season that's here.

Maker, Make Me (Four Prayers)
after Abigail Carroll

Make Me Water

Silver sluicing over stones
rush or trickle, cascade
percussion, silent acoustic
symphony, reflection in motion.
Rock and sand's victor,
channel etching a way
through at the lowest point.
All downhill, let me flow
freely towards the sea,
Source of all becoming.

Make Me Channel

Make me a channel changed
by seasons to drown the dryness,
drench arid canyons with chalked
and barren walls. Purging, coursing,
cleansing after Your flood, carve
and flow silver currents to quicken
thirst, send water where it wills.

Turn me towards hearts
empty of lifeblood, spilt
and split with broken hopes.
Glory me full to irrigate fallow
fields where Faith has seeded
yet nearly swept away by summer's
scorch and wind. Overflow my banks,
green my way, gracing fluid life

where hope lies just around the bend,
a raft of life to those in waiting.

Make Me Tree

Chlorophyll's engine returning
oxygen to earth, eternal
loop, gift of breathing.
Synthesis or magic, make
me leaves and bower,
shower-shaking, moisture-
making alchemy. Green
praise, wind waves
living towers raised,
made to fall in Your seasons.
Bring life in the losing,
laying down, letting go
to be re-leafed, cycle,
circle, sing again.

Make Me Bowl

Fired, gleaming, rounded vessel
In a quiet place, hollow for the
Holy to hear, perhaps reflect
His face. Silvered image to
hold and carry what would
sustain, rich meal of melody,
a song to the weary that they
might gain Heaven, poured out
in music over them. Feign
would I be empty, not
to fill, but resonate
and Thy tune to play.

Matins

I prayed for you this morning.
Slicing oranges, sunshine and
sugar coaxed from my hand.
Razor edge reminded me of care
needed to avoid the blade, careful
instead to ask for God's truest
cut through your heart
kindness holding drops of
sweetness to coax you
back to Him.

Looking Glass

Burgeoning day blanketed in
gray, a dome stretched
far and wide covers
this peace like quiet water.
Underneath, morning sounds
resonate the chamber—
bird song, a faraway horn, the
hello of my insistent clock.
Perhaps the subtle weathered
sides of sky are so much
batting, quilted in place
to hold us indoors or
urge us from beneath
the glass to be still.

Behold, both the yawning
of spring and riot of summer
on tomorrow's horizon.
Noisy revelations on
the other side of the glass
once we lift the lid
and fly.

Physical Science

Samara, she said and the words
took flight in my hearing,
invisible windborne flora
soaring across my thoughts.
She spoke of wings, a divine
creation spinning towards
earth to plant itself like a
stubborn weed—fierce and stuck.
Imagination took root,
sending me flying home
towards Webster's—
'some-are-uh'—and there
a black and white drawing of
a seed with wings
"an indehiscent, usually
one-seeded fruit, of the ash
or maple."

Like that spinning tree-gift
may I fly holy words,
carrying the seed of my
Savior to land, stuck
and stubborn, finally
splitting into silent roots
then skyward, bearing
fruit with wings.

Rain Sonnet

Liquid silver stream, muffled staccato
Plays while music rivulets, moistens earth,
A sonorous tune this gray summer's day.
Cloud-topped sun now hides in June's dull shadow
While we quiet ourselves and listen first
For what the meteoric language has to say.
Invisible tympani crashing now
On the heels of jagged flashing and bows
As an audience of two turns away
While fearing this horizon near to burst
With thunderous sermon both soft and low
Might split the Heavens with its sharps and flats
And leave the listeners each quaking and slow
While the powerful Conductor continues to play.

Real Time

Six o'clock sounds
say *hurry home!*
in the rush and whoosh
of tires sliding through
rain-soaked streets.
Digital dial confirms
the dinner hour
while a bird
outside my window
with his *cheerup, cheerup,
cheer!* reminds any and all
listeners evening
approaches soon.
Electronic *hmmzzz*
of the flat screen
insists I pay attention
to six o'clock news.

I resist the tell
and welcome instead
better clocks with
softer sounds—
the message bird calling,
the rainy streets memo
that day is done
and the drowsy way
I pen these words
at close of day.

Recipe for Awakening

Stir together singular,
disparate syllables.
Salt tears. Dry yeast.
Mix with water (no blood yet)
but sweat. *And all those tears.*
Beat, not with a spoon—convex
form no match for the fear held
in its hand—but carefully stir
the sifted self, Savior, kneaded
on a board until the dough
pulls away.
Cover loosely with cloth,
place in a battered space
until deliverance is complete.
Let rise.
Form into one life,
resurrected.

Revelation

Gather in your soul skin
like folds of a silken skirt.
Held close, fingered tight,
loosen it in time while
you eye the warp
and weft of fine
threads each a strand
of the cloth wrapped about you.

Unfurl at your choosing
as the Weaver beckons,
revealing bolts opulent
as pearl, iridescent,
multi-colored. Circling
your frame, the garment
sways as you dance
to music strummed
for those who swirl
the world in silken skirts.

To the Tune of Lilies

There is a song in petals,
rainsound of notes on thirsty
earth feeding spring's new flowers.
There is melody in garden-making
where silent, shriveled seeds
wait to burst, pushing mocha soil
with their magic strength.

There is harmony in golden
leafwhisper, silent shout
of green dusting tips
of dogwood, rose, tulip,
lilac, moss. Symphony grows
as God bouquets the earth
with color. We hear that distant
tune, resounding orchestra
and chorus calling us beyond
heavens to home.

True Wood

Pears thunk and plop on
    barren, yellow grass
    alone, not-gathered.
    The tree bore fruit
    but there is no one
    to eat of it.
    is it still a tree?
Upraised branches,
    so much verdant waterspray
    towards the sky,
    still and soft against
    the blue—
    but no one to see.
    is it still a tree?
Oaken limbs, worn with carrying children
    to and fro, pumping, playing
    jumping, but no one to
    hear the joy in the swing.
    is it still a tree?
Carpenter fashions these
    woodly beams,
    rough-hewn
    splinter-worthy
    dangerous to the flesh,
    carried for miles
    to the top of a hill-
    everyone sees—
    It was a tree.

Up

In the beginning begs the
existence of a dot, firstpoint
of a line referencing time
and movement, like an ant
crossing the Golden Gate.

If there is time
    we are here now
and movement
    subtle, but how?
why do we shun this guess
the size of a galaxy, turn from
the possibility of a God placing
each speck of us *just so?*

I may travel by antenna,
feel my way forward on small
steel and close pavement
stopping for crumbs.
But just because I cannot
see blue does not mean
there is no sky.

Wholly Spirit

No ordinary time this day
benchmarked by an evening
of fire, flaming tongues, God
come to Earth and men.
This morning marches towards
summer sun-ups unfolding one
after the other, sunsets pulling
the days forward. "Ordinary"
does not equal uniform, "without
consequence," "unremarkable."
No. I cling to that edge of burning,
its touch marking me with the
power of a Word on singed paper,
emblazoned brightness walking
me through all my days.

ACT III

SUMMER

MOVE & GROW

A Gift

Babies come in lumpy boxes, all
folded porcelain pudge, surprises
buried in gurgle, shriek and smile.
Experts have feigned understanding,
documenting stages, development,
what-to-expects along the way,
Sherlock-like. But they have no clue.
All the while in infant-speak, newborn
coos belie what's going on inside
those beribboned, noisy containers—
neurons firing in a multitude of synapses,
ligaments, sinew and bone growing
invisible and cell-deep in the dark.
Face it.
We know nothing now. We'll spend
the rest of our lives unwrapping the mystery.

A Capella

It's not the pull of green,
leafy cathedral embracing
this highway that magnets
me forward. It's the dream
of open sky calling through
turns as I travel the patchwork
pavement, a message of might be
and maybes, the perhaps of a
promise, places outside and above
these earthbound, hard-ground
wheels, reminding me of Somewhere
Else to be. A shore, a porch, a bench.

Half-notes and rests rise over
stoplights, across lanes, beyond
travelers, singing me far away.
So I fly.

Alchemy

Mint survives the frost
underground and flourishes
through ice and snow, a sudden
though stealthy return of greenburst
in the garden's sullen soil. Inklings
of fragrance creep along the
ground, announce sharpsweet
pungency as I crush newgreen
under my soles.

Each season's severity has little
effect on the vines' demise; I sigh
at their explosive, persistent
return and ponder gathering
the bounty of invasive
emeralds come June.
I'll rinse then steep then sip
steaming or iced, but only
after coaxing in the hottest
water. Perfume or palatable
drink, either way's a crucible.
Smashed and broken
or the slow roil, jadegreen
leaves change like straw
spun to gold, a sorcery
of sunshine and seasons.

Breath Prayer

In {breathe}
Pause {full}
Out {breathe}
Pause {empty}
Blood pumps with invisible
hands, red river flowing from
its source, enlivening limbs
returning like a never-full
sea, a cycle, a circle. Organ
played by the Spirit, pedals
pump and music pours
with songs or sighs. Still
we sing—empty notes but a
rest as red returns and
we breathe in.

Contrast: Second Peter Two

The difference between water and dust
is no simple verb declension, a shared
root of varied genesis. One springs forth
as moistured draughts, creation's
nourishment. The other, decay
and detritus trampled underfoot
and carried away on the wind.

Moving water flows from the fountained deep,
pours out music as it lands on thirsty hearts.

Dust is empty shells of seed, the stuffing
of clouds without water, good for filling nothing,
vapor that disappears without a trace.

I want to be water that stays.

Conversation

What did I do to deserve this?
is the wrong ask.
Because you didn't.
Do anything.

There is no quid pro quo / cash
economy in this wide, invisible
Kingdom-filled world.
Sunlight searching between oak
leaves, slant of green on birdbath,
chime of silver in the breeze. It's all gift.

Like the sloppy kiss of a two-year-old
or an unexpected letter in the mail,
you are worth surprising. Don't quibble
with your questions, paint your Creator
God as an if / then Savior. He is a because / when God.
Because you are mine, I will pour out
my gracelings when I want, to whom I want.
Just look up from time to time and say 'thanks.'
That is always the correct reply.

Flight Plan

I just saw three chickadees stun themselves,
Mama Bird watching from the patio post
hopeful their wings and wisdom
would coincide with the air.
They collided instead with the window,
the glass a surprise, barring flight and freedom,
impeding the discovery of their avian selves,
creatures made for God's pleasure and my joy.

Husband's kind hand cradles the weaker
of the two as tender, bending fingers
restore the feathery treasure.
Gentle, he tips his palm slightly
as spindly claws cling to this safe, sure place.
At last a tentative hop! to the railing
As the rattled Icarus rallies
and we hold our breath.
I turn and look back—
the bird has flown.

I marvel at the miracle of flight
and ponder the power
of a gentle touch that lifts
a sure hand that guides
and patience to push us
past safety to see if we can fly.

Gossamer Faith

Sir Spider suspended,
                    still
but for the invisible
jarring of his aerial
                    abode.
Does it frighten him
to be held by
strength he cannot see,

to scuttle across the
sky, limb to leaf
knowing the opposite
                    anchored
end could detach in a blink?

Still he spins in space,
hovers across my path
while I dodge and duck
and pray, *Dear God to have*
          faith of a spider.

Garden Ledger

Lavender linaria spikes upward,
miniature clouds stalk-perched
    as they reach for the sky.
Hummingbirds crowd-feed
    in the waning afternoon sun.
Carnations, red as a fresh-cut thumb,
    wave divine perfume from ruffled taffeta
    on gray-green stems.
Sweet peas' pungent surprise,
    a salmon / marshmallow palette,
    celestial bouquet a fragrance
    of that faraway gate in the Heavenlies.
Juncos chip-clacking in rhythm,
    sure-footed, clutch feeders
    afloat and trapeze in the breeze.
Leaves, light-transfigured day lanterns
    linger against a cornflower sky.
Voices ferried on the wind,
    gleeful hollers loud as a clap
    of thunder, neighborhood
    jazz accompaniment
    to the hushed afternoon.

Let the record show, no pockets
or wallets were emptied in exchange
for these riches, no bank account
tapped, no debt incurred to pay for this view.
The ledger will detail only this:
Full stop, eyes open, breathing slowed.
No currency noted but the bookkeeper's
scribe in a lazy hand,
Two slowing feet, arrested gaze, earful of sound.

The books are balanced and so is my soul.

Grandson, Summer

The raspberries—your favorite—ripened after
you'd gone, the sun's August denouement
leaving a subtle ruby postscript like pendants
suspended on green-edged strands.
Gentle tugs released the jewels between
my fingers then traveled to my mouth.
They were sweet (almost) and needed
more time for sugaring. Had you been here
to share the waning warm days' treasure
I could have held you, too, before you
grew into full-fledged bloom, walking into
the world seeking your own fruited fortune.

Sky Psalm, Toddler

What is this wonder on my skin?
Feathers drop; I drink it in. Downy
air drips and I blink up. Liquid
and blue touch, cool together and kiss
me—eyelash soft surprise. Eyes
wrinkle, crinkle at the wet. Droplets
glisten, dots of glass on grass as I
wave the liquid air, turning at the voice
telling me the word for this joy—
water.

Jewel Box

Trees shimmer and sway
in the breeze, branchy partners
against a Danube sky,
glassy diamonds on emerald
green. Arrow fragments shoot
skyward, golden waves
sounding their anthem.

A tune plays; ears and eyes register
song as it heralds the dawn of dusk.
Messages in light music lift notes
to the licorice sky while leaves
bend to sleep. Lilting lullaby
accompanies twilight dance,
ends with a bough.

On the Wind

His words breeze gently
moved by pinwheel's curve.
Iridescent blue shimmers
across surfaces, moves
the message gently
just within hearing, *I'm here.*
I ponder slowing—
less spin, more still—
like the quiet trees' hush
soft branches suspended
punctuation placed securely
on pages of sky, declaring
a full stop.

I've heard the music of His
kindness, long to be bathed
with Heaven's notes, lean in
and linger, strain for His
rumored voice. Cupping
His hand o'er my ear, He
shares secrets like a lover,
and I'm washed into waking,
shocked at the power
of quiet on the wind.

Pressed into Joy

Golden oil in
rounded vessel

liquid light
refracting sun in shimmers.

Mirrored shape
reflects on glassy surface

and I wonder at the
drop, drop, drops

of light as they
drip, drip, drip
down.

All this tasting
joyfulness because
something was crushed
and pressed,
leaving light.

Refining

What fires are blazing in faraway fields
where my life grows out of control?
What floods rage through the valleys
of my mind, washing away the life I've built?
What needs to go so that God can stay?

I ask for grace to see the refuse that wants
burning, eyes to see what should be swept away
in His timely storms while debris rushes by
and I'm left with empty spaces.
Bring the wind of your Spirit and build anew.
Fill the vacant land of my heart.

Ultrasound

Today we found out who you were
{who God was making you to be}
His poem in the womb—a verse
we can read for the rest of our lives.

Oatmeal cookies warmed in the oven
while I pondered garden tasks ahead—
sowing pregnant Cupani seeds towards the
promise of summer's sweetpea bounty,
blooming when you'd arrive, too.
Like the scent of surprise straight from
Heaven to us, characters in the story
God's been writing since time began.
We can't wait to meet you.

ACT IV

FALL

HARVEST & FUTURE

Steps to Picking Raspberries

First, avoid the bumblebees
zooming in for latent sugar
dripping in the rain, their heavy
soaking reflected in drops
from satiated rubies you hope
to pop in your mouth.

Second, beware the mildew, mold
and bursting moisture of berries
too long on the vine, having missed
the summer sun as you did, wondering
at the absent heat lo, these many months.

Third, cast a watchful gaze
at ubiquitous spiders who've homed
themselves midst the leaves, hiding
from the birds and maybe you. Their webs
give them away, as do the smattering
of mottled globes in the bottom
of your small bucket.

Lastly, swallow them, tiny yet tasty,
fresh and fruitful on this first day of Fall.

Age Is Just a Number

There is no statute of limitations on vision.
My old eyes register a darting messenger of
God's blatant, ineffable joy, watch the winged
creation hover in a web of air, spy a sleuthing
intruder snap-tapping its way across the wood,
tunneling his secret down the outside stairs.
No expiration (yet) for hearing.
Ears cataloguing birdvoice and the chipclacking
of breakfast at the feeder, morning's squeaking
insistence at the fountain.

Ever a student, teach me to number my days,
to register your Creator ways, the wind as it
ruffles the tablecloth in the morning's
gentle breeze, how cool, shortened
shadows signal this sea change
of a season rippling towards quieter times.
May I live this calendar daily,
not ticking towards the end and
its full stop, but aware and alive
and about Your business. No counting
lost hours, but living into Your
addition,
subtraction
multiplication,
division,
the only
math that matters.

Begin Again

September's singular day arrives with the turning
of many pages, paper or otherwise. Limbs of another
rich and growing year branch upward, leading
to vistas bright and unknown. I climb, grateful
for handholds, eyes on the open, azure sky.

Did Eden's first morning in that tree-filled glade
startle the couple awake, their eyes on a new dawn?
Burst with the gift of hope, that unknown need of a
fresh start? I say yes.

This new day, like that one, rich with possibilities
awaits as we journey. Now at a walk {or sometimes fly}
and fall, sure of a steady Hand to right us.
Our steps re-turned to the Kingdom, the sound
of that Voice birthed anew in the blazing
blue that calls towards home.

Celestial Bodies

—Ephesians 1:18–19

My weary eyes need reminders to
view the galaxies aright. Focused on
the sliver of moon, they forget an
entire orb hides in the dark.
I gaze at dull concrete, traipse
around the observatory, past
an entrance where God stands in the
doorway beckoning me to peer,
Galileo-like, past roofs, across
trees, into velvet sky.
As feet pause on sure ground,
a whisper beckons to dream
above, beyond to distant beauty.
Consider the immeasurable
heavens inside, reckon my
need as I'm handed a telescope.
Brightened eyes rest and remember.

Homing Orb

Sideways glancing, face atilt
she watches, wondering
at our wandering, solemnly
sees our not-seeing.

How do we miss it—
the faithful lumen bursting
barren emptiness, sun's reflection,
co-anchoring the sky?
Ignore her presence as she
pauses over our shoulder?

Nurturing nightlight, she whispers
to our worry, *Just Look Up*,
somberly sits in the quiet,
as mothers are wont to do,
waits for us to wonder anew,
bear witness to her faithfulness
and find our way home in the dark
by her gauzy light.

How to Be a Poem

God with us in the broken
place. E *manu* el, Yahweh
whose hand steadies and
steers us while we lift our face.
Prayers rise.
We cannot transform a heart
but we can tend and feed
the bodies housing hope,
care for roses, prune and
weed, wash and fold, clothe
the people who inhabit our
petitions.
Wholly Spirit, He is wholly
with us within, animates
our limbs to write His work
in the world through bread
and clothes, flower and song.
Be a maker.
Be a prayer.
Be a poem.

I Choose

The faith of eggs, cream, lemon,
sugar to spin into ribbons,
meet with butter, flour, leavening
and become a layered, luxurious cake.
I choose to imagine that simple
single ingredients, disparate,
divided, alone, would
choose to leave the safety of
the cupboard, pantry or fridge
and leap (with assistance)
at the chance to become
something. Anything.
Except alone, disparate, divided.
I choose to believe
That left alone in the dark
long enough, anyone who sees
a single, soft beam would move
towards the gleam, leave their
darkness and choose to be spun
into golden life.

Night. Time.

Owl's dark tremolo murmurs like an airborne
river, pauses as it bends on the wind.
I hold my breath, capture the creature's
call while it vanishes unheard and I hurry
past. Curiosity lures me onward, deepens
attention. I pause mid-step, sound settles,
voice-rich on velvet night while I sigh
at the current noises calling me inside
and away from the sky's music. Still,
the sound weaves through the night
between panes, deep underwater,
a symphony on the evening's breeze.

ACT V

COMING
& GOING

Father/Falter

Sunday nights I'd feign sleep carpetside
surrounded by siblings, three feet from the
television. The Wide World of Disney faded from
the screen, its signature theme song ebbing
beneath the waves of my almost-dreams.
I wanted to be held, carried in the bridge
of my father's arms, close in those moments
of me-only-and-no-one-else, praying
the memory would stay more than skin deep.

My pretensions often worked, the bridge holding
but only just. His reach slowly gave way
and memories vanished as lost years spanned
the distance between each shore.
Slowly he lost sight of us, gaze leading
him away, ambling towards other arms.
Out of reach and across the years, he turned
towards a home not ours, holding only
himself and a broken heart.
He never crossed over again.

Gilt Gift

Sometimes I guilt myself right out
of joy. Like the surprise of an iridescent
butterfly from an unsightly cocoon,
who would expect this shimmering
show in morning sunlight?
Eyes are trained on Northwest firs
framed in blue, frosted feeders,
feathered presents hidden among
the trees.

I've held my breath, wondering.
Did my mother ever ponder stilling
herself, take a moment with the
birds in her California garden? Gaze
restful at morning fog carried
in on marine air? Was she ever at ease
in her troubled life, as she parented
us alone?
I will never know.
I cannot ring her up to ask, there
is no email to send, no letter to write.
She is gone, stolen far too soon.

I consider this feigned injustice.
How wildly unfair I should gather
such beauty as surely she never did,
then abandon my thoughts. No.
I will not leave reason to balance the
ledger, steal this away, too. Feathered
hum of heat, filigreed pane, frosty view.
I drink in sleeping green, hear her
whisper over my shoulder,
Breathe in the brilliant morning.
Surrender second guesses and leave
logic to the philosophers.

I startle to the present, welcome with
wonder this gilt gift, nothing to ponder
but my thanks.

The Scarlet Cord

There was no faithline or family
promises passed on through prayer.
Only a bloodline from Creation's
start, scarlet thread bound and
wound together, a cord the color of life
made by a Weaver who dyed it red
with blood. Woven with the loom
of love, a lifeline coming my way~
over the wall and bright enough
for me to see, alone and far away
like Rahab's spies. Salvation's
sign let down from Heaven, life ring
through the air, a grasp of new
grace as I welcomed my Omnipresent
Pursuer. No earthly reason to be
ushered in save for God sending a sign
to this wanderer in the land of Jericho.

Hand Made

I bend to be formed,
not torn or broken
but tempered by heat,
a fire so hot the glow
is all You see of me.
I said *change* and *grow*
and I'm bent so low
this shape of me is
melting brass forged
by tools so strong
I fear the breaking.

But I'm bound to bend,
be shaped, sheared sound,
let this shine of me
play gleaming glory,
become the beautiful
breath of sudden
notes quickened by
Spirit, living tune played
through me, a golden
song borne on the
honeyed breeze of dawn.

What My Grandkids Will Say About Me on Oprah

When my grandkids talk to Oprah
    about their Nana, *the famous writer,*
they will say words were my oxygen—
    to read, write and share
and that I spent way too much money
    at thrift stores on books by dead authors—
Emily Dickinson, George Herbert, L. M. Montgomery
    and Keats.

They will also tell her I loved to sing—
    another form of breathing—
and how I embarrassed them in public
    by belting out the "Tomorrow" song from Annie
or grabbing their elbows in the mall
    while shouting "We're off to see the Wizard!"

They will announce to the world,
    in front of God and everybody,
that my profession as a teacher was their
    greatest undoing; constantly coaching
about penmanship, the correct formation
of the letter "a," pointing out misread
syllables in a favorite text.

They will oblige Ms. O's prodding by adding the death
    knell—
that I couldn't help myself when it came to learning,
    revealing in hushed tones that I often resorted
to using an encyclopedia as torture
    (the 1956 World Book edition).

My grandchildren will remind her, however,
    (before the commercial break)
my best qualities were the way I delighted in the world,
    showing them wonders in the garden,
surprises in the grass, the avian miracles of
    chickadees and juncos in the branches,
    robins in the birdbath.

Most of all, when my grandkids talk to Oprah,
    they will tell her my lungs longed for the breath of
    Heaven, the Word, and how its oxygen proved
    my greatest life support throughout my livelong days.

ACKNOWLEDGMENTS

Grateful acknowledgment is given to the following publications, both print and online, where some of these poems first appeared: *BarrenMag*, "After Clarice"; *Altarwork*, "Revelation"; *The Joyful Life Magazine*, "Alchemy"; *iolamag*, "Pressed into Joy"; *Awake Our Hearts*, "Gilt Gift"; *Ephesians Poetry Project-D. S. Martin, Ed.*, "Celestial Bodies"; *Refine Journal*, "Pilgrimage" and *Salt & Clay Summer 2020*, "Garden Ledger."

A hundred thanks go to all my cheerleaders and support team who encouraged me in this endeavor, particularly K. C. Ireton, whose astute observations of the text have been a gift. I am especially grateful to the early readers who agreed to read *Hearts on Pilgrimage* and say nice things about the work—Laura Boggess, Laura Kauffman, Glynn Young, Shawn Smucker, Sandra Heska King, Kelly Chripczuk, Elizabeth Marshall and Kim Hyland—thank you.

To my launch team: Ana Lisa de Jong, Anita Palmer, Gina Ellis, Carol Wilson, Gwen McIntosh, Karin Fendick, Kelly Greer, Meagan Davenport, Melody Schwarting, Michele Morin, Natalie Ogbourne, Rachael Denny, Shara-Rae Jensen and Briana Almengor for your parts, both big and small, please accept my round of applause.

To my blog readers, social media friends and followers, God bless you for following the trail of my birdseed across screens and in person. Your presence means so very much and I'm grateful for each one of you.

One person in particular whose inspiration is woven underneath and throughout this work is L. L. Barkat, founder of Tweetspeak Poetry. When I started writing online in

2012, I sent her an email full of questions about my new adventure in blogging, to which she graciously replied. Because of the magic of virtual connections, I extended an invitation to Barkat and her traveling Mischief Café, which arrived in my Seattle dining room one lovely night in November 2014. There was poetry reading, toast and tea (and feather boas!). I would never have considered myself a poet if it weren't for L. L. Note: "I Choose" on page 74 is a direct response to a prompt in Tweetspeak's Mischief Café book. (More at tweetspeakpoetry.com.)

My grandchildren have asked me often about whether I'm a famous author yet, "even though not too many people read poetry, Nana." (I hope to prove them otherwise with the book you now hold in your hands.) Oldest to youngest, they all inspire some of my best poems, many of which are woven into these pages.

My very patient and precious husband Bill has cheered me on, even though he just "doesn't get poetry." Thank you, honey, for letting me ignore you while I typed like a madwoman and for bragging about my work to anyone who'll listen. I love you dearly.

Made in the USA
Monee, IL
08 January 2021